THE ARV ESTIMATION BLUEPRINT

A Comprehensive Guide To ARV Mastery

Dack Douglas

Icon Publications Limited

INTRODUCTION

Welcome to the captivating world of real estate valuation, where the art of estimating After Repair Value (ARV) takes center stage. Whether you're a seasoned investor seeking to fine-tune your valuation skills or a newcomer eager to navigate the labyrinth of property assessment, this book is your essential guide to mastering ARV like the pros.

Picture this: you stand before a property, envisioning its transformation from a diamond in the rough to a prized gem in the market. Your ability to accurately gauge its post-renovation value isn't just a skill; it's a superpower that empowers you to make informed decisions, seize opportunities, and unlock the full potential of real estate investments.

As you embark on this enlightening journey, you'll delve into the intricate world of ARV estimation, unraveling the threads that connect market trends, property features, and renovation magic. Here, we demystify the techniques employed by industry experts, lifting the veil on their strategies and empowering you to apply their wisdom to your own ventures.

But this isn't just a theoretical exploration. No, it's a hands-on experience that immerses you in the world of real-world case studies, practical exercises, and insightful anecdotes. We believe that the true power of ARV estimation lies not just in formulas and data, but in your ability to grasp the nuances, adjust for variables, and harness the forces that shape property values.

Your journey begins here, as we embark on a quest to unravel the secrets of ARV estimation, unveil the artistry behind valuation methodologies, and equip you with the knowledge and tools to estimate ARV like the seasoned pros. Get ready to embark on a voyage of discovery, enrichment, and empowerment—one that will forever change the way you view, assess, and elevate real estate investments. Let's dive in and unlock the potential of ARV estimation, igniting your journey to becoming a true master of property valuation.

CONTENTS

Chapter 6: Considering Property Features and Upgrades

How property features affect ARV
Valuing renovations and upgrades effectively
Calculating ROI on improvement projects

Chapter 7: Handling Special Cases and Challenges

Dealing with unique property types
Estimating ARV for distressed properties
Addressing complex scenarios and limitations

Chapter 8: The Role of Appraisals

Understanding the appraisal process and its connection to ARV
Leveraging appraisals for accurate ARV estimation
Collaborating with appraisers effectively

Chapter 9: Fine-Tuning Your ARV Estimation Skills

Continuous learning and staying updated on market trends
Refining your estimation techniques over time
Avoiding common pitfalls and mistakes

Chapter 10: Applying ARV in Real Estate Ventures

Integrating ARV estimation into investment decisions
Negotiation strategies based on ARV insights
Real-world success stories and case studies
This original outline provides a comprehensive structure for your book, covering the fundamental concepts of ARV estimation, data collection, comparative analysis, market trends, property features, challenges, appraisals, skill development, and practical application in real estate endeavors.

CHAPTER 1: INTRODUCTION TO ARV ESTIMATION

Understanding The Significance Of ARV In Real Estate

To grasp the importance of After Repair Value (ARV) in the realm of real estate, one must delve into its core significance. ARV stands as a pivotal metric, embodying the estimated value a property attains following necessary repairs and enhancements. This figure is pivotal for investors and sellers alike, offering a compass that guides decisions on pricing, investments, and potential profits. Understanding ARV involves a comprehensive analysis of property condition, comparable sales, and market trends, enabling stakeholders to accurately gauge a property's post-renovation worth. As a cornerstone of real estate strategy, a keen comprehension of ARV empowers individuals to make informed choices, ensuring optimal returns on investments and informed negotiations within the dynamic landscape of property transactions.

Role Of Arv In Property Investment And Flipping

The role of After Repair Value (ARV) in property investment and flipping is pivotal and multifaceted. ARV serves as a guiding beacon for investors and flippers, offering a clear and calculated perspective on the potential value a property can attain after undergoing necessary repairs and renovations. This metric serves as a cornerstone for strategic decision-making, influencing critical aspects of the investment process.

For property investors, ARV provides an essential framework for assessing the viability of a potential investment. By accurately estimating the post-repair value, investors can gauge the potential return on investment (ROI) and make informed choices about whether a property aligns with their financial goals. ARV helps investors weigh the costs of renovations against the anticipated increase in property value, thereby enabling them to allocate resources effectively and minimize risks.

In the context of property flipping, ARV plays a central role in determining the profitability of the venture. Flippers rely on ARV to guide their purchase decisions, renovation budgets, and sales strategies. By comprehending the post-renovation value, flippers can strategize their improvements to maximize the property's appeal and marketability, ultimately leading to a higher resale price.

In essence, ARV acts as a compass that navigates property investment and flipping endeavors. It empowers investors and flippers to make informed choices, optimize their financial outcomes, and navigate the intricate landscape of real estate transactions with a calculated approach.

Setting The Foundation For Accurate ARV Estimation

Establishing a solid foundation for accurate After Repair Value (ARV) estimation in real estate hinges upon a systematic and comprehensive approach. To achieve this, several key steps are crucial:

Comparable Sales Analysis: Conduct a thorough examination of recent sales data for properties similar in size, location, and condition to the subject property. This comparative analysis provides valuable insights into market trends and helps establish a baseline for estimating the property's potential value post-repair.

Property Inspection: A meticulous inspection of the subject property is imperative. Identify any needed repairs or renovations that could enhance its value. Accurate assessment of the property's current condition lays the groundwork for calculating the value it could attain after improvements.

Local Market Research: Delve into the local real estate market dynamics. Understand factors such as demand, supply, neighborhood trends, and amenities that influence property values. This contextual understanding is vital in gauging how renovations might impact ARV.

Consultation with Professionals: Seek insights from real estate agents, appraisers, and contractors with local expertise. Their knowledge can shed light on the potential value enhancement achievable through specific renovations and upgrades.

Renovation Budgeting: Develop a detailed budget for the repairs and improvements needed to elevate the property's condition. Precise budgeting allows for accurate cost projections and helps avoid overestimating or underestimating potential ARV.

Consideration of Market Conditions: Be attuned to current market conditions, as they can significantly influence property values. A fluctuating market may necessitate adjustments to ARV estimates based on shifting buyer preferences and demand.

Future Market Projections: Anticipate future market trends and potential shifts. A forward-looking approach to ARV estimation incorporates long-term considerations that may impact the property's value over time.

Use of Technology: Leverage real estate valuation tools, software, and online platforms to streamline data collection and analysis. These resources can aid in generating more accurate ARV estimates based on historical and current data.

By diligently following these steps, real estate professionals and investors can lay the groundwork for precise ARV estimation. This process ensures a well-informed approach to property valuation, leading to confident decision-making and successful outcomes in the dynamic landscape of real estate transactions.

* * *

CHAPTER 2: THE BASICS OF PROPERTY VALUATION

Exploring Different Property Valuation Methods

Exploring various property valuation methods involves a deliberate and systematic approach to gaining a comprehensive understanding of a property's worth. To embark on this journey effectively, consider the following steps:

Research and Education: Begin by acquainting yourself with the fundamental principles of property valuation. Study different methods, their strengths, limitations, and when they are most appropriate. This foundational knowledge will guide your exploration.

Diverse Valuation Approaches: Familiarize yourself with a range of valuation methods, including Comparative Market Analysis (CMA), Income Capitalization, Cost Approach, and the Sales Comparison Approach. Each method offers a distinct perspective on property value based on factors such as market data, income potential, and replacement cost.

Practical Application: Apply each valuation method to real-world scenarios. Select properties with varying characteristics and use the appropriate method to estimate their value. This hands-on practice enhances your ability to assess the relevance and accuracy of each approach.

Case Studies: Analyze case studies and real-life examples where different valuation methods were employed. Examine how each method yielded results and understand the rationale behind the chosen approach in specific situations.

Consult Experts: Engage with real estate professionals, appraisers, and experienced investors. Their insights and practical experiences can provide valuable perspectives on when and how to employ specific valuation methods effectively.

Technology and Tools: Utilize modern technology and valuation tools to streamline the process. Online calculators, software, and databases can expedite data collection and analysis across different methods.

Continual Learning: Stay abreast of evolving trends in property valuation. Attend workshops, webinars, and seminars to deepen your knowledge and learn about emerging valuation techniques.

Comparative Analysis: Conduct side-by-side comparisons of the results obtained from various valuation methods for the same property. This comparative analysis helps you grasp the nuances of each method and their implications on property value interpretation.

Network and Discussion: Engage in discussions with peers and experts in the real estate industry. Collaborative conversations can provide fresh insights, alternative perspectives, and a deeper understanding of the nuances inherent in property valuation.

Practice and Feedback: Regularly practice applying different valuation methods and seek feedback from experienced professionals. Constructive feedback can guide your refinement of valuation skills and enhance your accuracy over time.

By embracing these steps, you can embark on a comprehensive exploration of property valuation methods. This journey equips you with a versatile skill set, enabling you to adeptly evaluate properties from multiple angles and make informed decisions within the intricate realm of real estate valuation.

Comparative Market Analysis (CMA) And Its Relevance To ARV

Comparative Market Analysis (CMA) is a fundamental tool in the realm of real estate that plays a pivotal role in determining property values, including the After Repair Value (ARV). CMA involves a systematic evaluation of recently sold, active, and pending properties within a specific geographic area, which share similarities with the subject property in terms of location, size, condition, and features.

Relevance to ARV and Real Estate:

Property Valuation: CMA provides valuable insights into the current market conditions by analyzing comparable properties. This information is essential for estimating a property's value, especially when considering renovations for the purpose of enhancing ARV. The analysis of comparable properties' sales prices offers a realistic benchmark against which the potential value of a renovated property can be gauged.

Renovation Decision-Making: For real estate investors and flippers, CMA aids in making informed decisions about which renovations or improvements will yield the highest returns. By assessing how various features impact the selling prices of comparable properties, investors can strategically allocate resources to enhance a property's appeal and maximize ARV.

Market Trends: CMA sheds light on trends and shifts in the local real estate market. Investors can identify patterns in property values, such as seasonal fluctuations or changing buyer preferences. This insight is vital when projecting the potential ARV and making timing-sensitive decisions.

Pricing Strategy: Real estate agents often use CMA to recommend an appropriate listing price for a property. When estimating ARV, this same approach helps flippers and investors determine a competitive resale price that aligns with market realities, ensuring a quicker sale and optimal returns.

Negotiation: CMA supports negotiation strategies by providing objective data to support pricing discussions. Both buyers and sellers can use CMA-derived information to substantiate their respective positions during negotiations related to the ARV and property value.

Risk Management: CMA assists in assessing the risk associated with property investment. By understanding how similar properties have fared in terms of sales prices and market demand, investors can make calculated decisions to mitigate potential risks when estimating ARV.

In essence, Comparative Market Analysis is a cornerstone of real estate valuation, including the determination of After Repair Value. It enables stakeholders to make informed decisions based on factual data, enhances accuracy in property valuation, and supports strategic choices in the dynamic landscape of real estate transactions.

Factors That Influence Property Values

Residential property values are influenced by a multitude of factors that collectively shape the perceived worth of a property within the real estate market. These factors are diverse and interrelated, playing a crucial role in determining a property's market value:

Location: The geographic positioning of a property is paramount. Proximity to amenities, schools, transportation hubs, and desirable neighborhoods significantly impacts property values.

Property Size and Layout: The size of the property, both land and building, along with its layout, number of bedrooms, bathrooms, and overall livable space, contribute to its value.

Condition and Age: The overall condition of the property and its age influence value. Well-maintained properties and those with modern amenities tend to command higher prices.

Comparative Market Analysis (CMA): The recent sales prices of similar properties in the vicinity, as revealed by CMA, provide a benchmark for property values.

Market Demand and Supply: The balance between the demand for housing and the availability of properties for sale in a given area affects property values. High demand and limited supply tend to drive values up.

Economic Factors: The overall economic health of an area, including employment opportunities, income levels, and economic growth, impacts property values.

Interest Rates: Fluctuations in mortgage interest rates can affect buyers' purchasing power and, subsequently, property demand and values.

Neighborhood Trends: Property values are influenced by the desirability and trends within the neighborhood, including crime rates, community development, and lifestyle amenities.

School District Quality: Properties located within highly rated school districts tend to attract higher demand and, consequently, higher property values.

Infrastructure and Development: Planned or ongoing infrastructure projects, such as transportation improvements or commercial developments, can influence property values positively.

Property Features: Unique features such as a view, outdoor space, swimming pool, or energy-efficient upgrades can enhance a property's value.

Economic Stability: The stability of the local and national economy can affect consumer confidence and influence property values.

Property Zoning and Regulations: Zoning laws, building regulations, and local ordinances can impact property values by limiting development potential or affecting property use.

Environmental Factors: Proximity to natural resources, parks, bodies of water, and potential environmental hazards can influence property values.

Market Perception: Public perception and sentiment about an area can influence demand, thereby affecting property values.

These factors, among others, interact to determine residential property values. Understanding their dynamics is crucial for property buyers, sellers, investors, and real estate professionals to make informed decisions within the complex landscape of real estate transactions.

* * *

CHAPTER 3: GATHERING DATA AND INFORMATION

Essential Data Points For Accurate ARV Estimation

Accurate After Repair Value (ARV) estimation in residential real estate relies on gathering and analyzing essential data points that collectively paint a comprehensive picture of a property's potential value post-renovation. Key data points to consider include:

Comparative Sales: Recent sales prices of comparable properties in the same neighborhood or vicinity provide a direct benchmark for estimating ARV.

Property Details: Accurate information about the property's size, layout, number of bedrooms, bathrooms, and other features is essential for precise valuation.

Renovation Costs: A detailed breakdown of anticipated renovation costs helps determine how upgrades will impact the property's value.

Local Market Trends: Insights into current market conditions, including demand, supply, and recent trends, guide ARV estimation.

Neighborhood Desirability: Information about the neighborhood's amenities, school quality, safety, and overall desirability affects property values.

Comparable Features: Identifying similar properties with comparable features and condition ensures a relevant basis for ARV calculation.

Property Condition: An accurate assessment of the property's current state, including necessary repairs and improvements, is vital for projecting its potential value.

Historical Data: Historical data on property sales and price trends offer insights into how the market has evolved over time.

Local Economic Factors: Consider the local economic climate, job growth, and other economic indicators that influence property demand and value.

Future Development: Awareness of planned or potential future developments in the area can impact the property's long-term value.

Local Regulations: Knowledge of zoning laws, building codes, and other regulations that may affect property use and value.

Comparable Property Features: Identifying comparable properties with similar features, such as lot size, style, and amenities, ensures a more accurate valuation.

Property History: Understanding the property's sales history and any previous renovations can provide insights into its value trajectory.

Market Seasonality: Recognizing seasonal fluctuations in property demand and sales can help adjust ARV estimates accordingly.

Investor Perspective: Factoring in an investor's expected return on investment (ROI) helps align ARV estimation with investment goals.

Professional Input: Consulting real estate agents, appraisers, and industry experts can provide valuable insights and validation of ARV estimates.

Property Age and Upgrades: Information about the property's age and recent upgrades helps assess its appeal and condition.

By diligently collecting and analyzing these essential data points, real estate professionals and investors can enhance the accuracy of their ARV estimations, leading to more informed decision-making and successful outcomes in residential real estate ventures.

Accessing Real Estate Databases And Online Tools

Accessing real estate databases and online tools requires a strategic approach that empowers you to gather valuable insights and make informed decisions within the dynamic realm of real estate. Here's a step-by-step guide on how to navigate this process effectively:

Research and Identify Tools: Begin by researching and identifying reputable real estate databases and online tools. Look for platforms that provide comprehensive property data, market trends, and analytical features. Popular options include Zillow, Redfin, Realtor.com, and local Multiple Listing Services (MLS) platforms.

User Registration: Create accounts on the selected platforms. Registration may be free or require a subscription, depending on the level of access and features you need.

Navigation and Familiarization: Take time to navigate and familiarize yourself with the interface and functionalities of each platform. Explore search options, filters, and data categories available.

Property Search: Utilize search features to explore properties in your target areas. Refine your search based on criteria such as location, property type, price range, and features.

Property Details: Dive into property details, including listing descriptions, photos, and virtual tours. Pay attention to key information that aligns with your investment or buying criteria.

Comparable Sales: Look for tools or sections that provide information on comparable sales (comps) in the area. Analyze recent sales prices of properties similar to your subject property to gauge market trends.

Market Trends and Data: Access market trend reports, historical price data, and local real estate statistics. These insights help you understand how property values have evolved over time.

Financial Calculators: Many platforms offer calculators to estimate mortgage payments, property taxes, and potential returns on investment. These tools assist in evaluating the financial aspects of a property.

Community Information: Explore data on schools, crime rates, demographics, and amenities in the neighborhood. Understanding the local community adds context to your property analysis.

Virtual Tours and Maps: Take advantage of virtual tours, property maps, and satellite imagery to visually assess properties and their surroundings.

Real Estate Forums and Blogs: Many online platforms host forums and blogs where users share insights, tips, and experiences related to real estate. Participate in discussions and seek advice from fellow investors or professionals.

Mobile Apps: Some platforms offer mobile apps for on-the-go access. Download and use these apps to stay connected and make quick property inquiries.

Networking: Connect with real estate professionals, agents, and investors through online platforms. Networking can provide valuable information and potential collaboration opportunities.

Data Verification: While online tools are valuable, cross-reference data with multiple sources and consider consulting local experts for verification.

Continual Learning: Stay updated with platform enhancements, new tools, and emerging trends in real estate technology. Regularly explore new features that could enhance your property analysis.

By following these steps, you can effectively access real estate databases and online tools, harnessing their capabilities to streamline your property research, analysis, and decision-making processes within the dynamic world of real estate.

Networking With Local Agents And Appraisers

Building meaningful connections with local real estate agents and appraisers involves a strategic and respectful approach that fosters genuine relationships. Here's a step-by-step guide on how to effectively network with these professionals:

Research and Identify: Begin by researching and identifying reputable real estate agents and appraisers in your local area. Look for individuals with a strong track record, positive reviews, and a deep understanding of the local real estate market.

Attend Networking Events: Attend local real estate seminars, workshops, conferences, and industry events. These gatherings provide opportunities to meet and connect with professionals face-to-face.

Online Presence: Connect with real estate agents and appraisers on professional networking platforms like LinkedIn. Engage with their posts, share relevant content, and send personalized connection requests.

Introduction: Reach out with a personalized and courteous introduction, expressing your interest in connecting and learning from their expertise.

Offer Value: Approach the relationship with a mindset of giving before receiving. Offer to share your insights, collaborate on projects, or provide assistance that aligns with their needs.

Seek Advice: Express your eagerness to learn and seek advice from their experience. Pose thoughtful questions and demonstrate your genuine interest in their insights.

Coffee Meetings: Propose informal coffee meetings or virtual calls to discuss industry trends, market insights, or specific property inquiries. Such meetings create a relaxed environment for knowledge exchange.

Attend Open Houses: Attend open houses hosted by local real estate agents. This provides an opportunity to meet them in a more casual setting and discuss properties and market trends.

Referral Exchange: Be open to referring clients to real estate agents and appraisers when appropriate. This fosters goodwill and can lead to reciprocal referrals in the future.

Collaborative Projects: Explore opportunities for collaboration, such as joint property analysis, market research, or investment ventures. Collaborative efforts can solidify relationships.

Local Chambers of Commerce: Participate in local business networking groups or chambers of commerce events. These platforms provide a diverse network of professionals to connect with.

Real Estate Associations: Join local real estate associations or clubs. These groups offer a forum for networking, education, and sharing insights with fellow industry members.

Follow-Up: After initial interactions, follow up with a thank-you note or email expressing appreciation for their time and insights. Stay engaged by periodically sharing relevant updates or resources.

Stay Respectful: Respect their time and boundaries. Approach networking with a genuine intention, avoiding excessive self-promotion or demands.

Continuous Engagement: Networking is an ongoing process. Nurture relationships by staying in touch, offering assistance, and demonstrating your commitment to the relationship over time.

By following these steps, you can cultivate meaningful connections with local real estate agents and appraisers, fostering a network of professionals who can provide valuable insights, guidance, and collaboration opportunities in the dynamic field of real estate.

* * *

CHAPTER 4: THE ART OF COMPARATIVE ANALYSIS

Step-By-Step Guide To Conducting A Comprehensive Comparative Market Analysis

Conducting a comprehensive Comparative Market Analysis (CMA) involves a structured approach to gather and analyze data, ultimately providing valuable insights into property values. Here's a step-by-step guide to conducting a thorough CMA:

Define Your Scope: Clearly define the scope of your analysis, including the property type (e.g., single-family home, condo), location, and timeframe (recent sales within the past few months).

Gather Property Details: Collect detailed information about the subject property, including its size, layout, number of bedrooms, bathrooms, and any unique features.

Select Comparable Properties: Identify recently sold properties that are similar to the subject property in terms of location, size, condition, and features. Aim for a mix of active, pending, and sold listings.

Compile Data: Gather data on each comparable property, including sale prices, listing prices, days on market, property condition, and features. You can use online real estate databases, MLS systems, and local property records for this information.

Adjustment Factors: Identify key differences between the subject property and each comparable property. Common adjustment factors include square footage, additional features (e.g., pool, garage), and condition. Apply positive or negative adjustments to the comparable properties' sale prices based on these differences.

Calculate Adjusted Values: Apply the adjustment factors to the comparable properties' sale prices to calculate their adjusted values. This helps normalize the data and create a more accurate comparison.

Weighted Analysis: Assign weights to each comparable property based on factors like proximity, similarity, and recentness. Calculate a weighted average of the adjusted values to arrive at an estimated value for the subject property.

Market Trends: Research local market trends, such as supply and demand dynamics, changes in property values, and any external factors that could influence the market.

Prepare CMA Report: Create a comprehensive CMA report that includes the subject property details, a list of comparable properties, their adjusted values, adjustments made, and the estimated value range for the subject property.

Analyze Results: Interpret the results of your CMA analysis. Compare the estimated value range with other valuation methods, such as the Income Capitalization Approach or Cost Approach, if applicable.

Consider External Factors: Factor in additional considerations that could impact the property's value, such as neighborhood desirability, school quality, and local economic conditions.

Present Findings: If you're a real estate professional, present your CMA findings to clients in a clear and understandable manner. Explain the rationale behind adjustments and provide insights into the local market.

Stay Updated: As market conditions change, periodically update your CMA analysis to reflect the latest data and trends.

By following these steps, you can conduct a comprehensive Comparative Market Analysis that provides a well-informed estimate of a property's value based on current market dynamics and the characteristics of comparable properties.

Selecting Appropriate Comparable Properties

Selecting appropriate comparable properties for a Comparative Market Analysis (CMA) requires a thoughtful and methodical approach to ensure accuracy and relevancy. Here's a step-by-step guide on how to choose the most suitable comparables:

Define Criteria: Clearly define the criteria that align with the subject property. Consider factors such as location, property type (e.g., single-family home, condo), size, layout, number of bedrooms, bathrooms, and essential features.

Geographic Proximity: Prioritize properties within the same neighborhood or immediate vicinity as the subject property. The closer the comparables are, the more accurate the analysis.

Similarity: Choose properties that closely resemble the subject property in terms of size, layout, architectural style, and overall design. Look for comparables that reflect the same property characteristics.

Recent Sales: Focus on recently sold properties within the past few months. Properties with outdated sales data may not accurately reflect current market conditions.

Similar Condition: Opt for comparables that share a similar level of condition with the subject property. Properties in similar states of repair provide a more accurate basis for valuation.

Comparable Features: Identify properties with comparable features, such as a similar number of bedrooms, bathrooms, and essential amenities (e.g., garage, pool, view).

Property Type: Choose comparables that are the same property type as the subject property. For example, compare single-family homes with other single-family homes, and condos with other condos.

Size Matching: Pay attention to square footage and lot size. Properties with similar dimensions contribute to a more accurate valuation.

Sales Date: Select properties that have sold recently to reflect the most up-to-date market conditions. Avoid using outdated sales data that might not align with the current market trends.

Comparable Sales: Look for properties that have sold, rather than properties that are currently listed or pending. Sold properties provide concrete data on actual transaction prices.

Exclude Outliers: Remove any outliers or atypical properties that significantly deviate from the subject property's characteristics or market conditions.

Data Accuracy: Verify the accuracy of property data, sale prices, and transaction details for each comparable. Rely on reliable sources such as MLS listings or official property records.

Variety: Aim for a mix of comparables that cover a range of sale prices. Including both higher and lower-priced properties helps establish a more balanced valuation range.

Market Trends: Consider current market trends and any recent shifts in property values when selecting comparables.

Professional Insight: If you're uncertain, seek input from experienced real estate agents or appraisers who have a deep understanding of the local market.

By adhering to these steps, you can systematically select appropriate comparable properties that closely align with the subject property, enhancing the accuracy and reliability of your Comparative Market Analysis.

Adjusting For Differences And Variations

Effectively adjusting for differences and variations in a Comparative Market Analysis (CMA) involves a methodical approach that ensures a fair and accurate comparison between the subject property and comparable properties. Here's a step-by-step guide on how to make adjustments:

Identify Key Differences: Begin by identifying the key differences between the subject property and each comparable property. Factors such as square footage, number of bedrooms, bathrooms, and notable features should be considered.

Determine Adjustments: For each identified difference, determine whether it positively or negatively affects the value of the comparable property compared to the subject property. Assign a dollar value to the adjustment based on market knowledge, historical data, and expert opinion.

Quantify Adjustments: Quantify adjustments in monetary terms. For example, if a comparable property has an additional bedroom compared to the subject property, estimate how much that extra bedroom adds to its value.

Use Common Factors: Identify common factors that frequently require adjustments, such as square footage, lot size, condition, location, view, amenities, and upgrades.

Percentage Adjustments: Consider using percentage adjustments for certain factors. For instance, a larger property might have a higher percentage adjustment for square footage compared to a smaller property.

Regression Analysis: Utilize regression analysis or statistical tools to analyze the relationship between specific property features and their impact on sale prices. This can provide a more data-driven approach to making adjustments.

Comparable Match: Seek out comparable properties that closely match the subject property in terms of characteristics. The more similar the comparables, the fewer adjustments needed.

Cumulative Adjustments: If multiple differences exist, make cumulative adjustments by adding or subtracting the individual adjustments to arrive at a total adjustment value for each comparable.

Sensitivity Analysis: Conduct a sensitivity analysis to assess the impact of adjustments on the final valuation. Test different adjustment values to understand how they influence the estimated value range.

Expert Consultation: Consult with experienced real estate professionals or appraisers to validate and refine your adjustments. Their insights can provide a more accurate perspective on the value impact of specific differences.

Documentation: Clearly document each adjustment made, explaining the rationale behind it. This transparency ensures transparency and supports the credibility of your CMA analysis.

Range of Adjustments: If there is a range of possible adjustments, present a range of estimated values to account for varying scenarios.

Review and Refinement: Continuously review and refine your adjustment process based on feedback, market trends, and evolving real estate conditions.

By adhering to these steps, you can navigate the intricacies of adjusting for differences and variations in a Comparative Market Analysis, resulting in a more precise and credible assessment of the subject property's value relative to the comparables.

* * *

CHAPTER 5: EVALUATING MARKET TRENDS

Identifying And Interpreting Local Market Trends

Identifying and interpreting local market trends in residential real estate involves a comprehensive approach that empowers you to make informed decisions within the dynamic real estate landscape. Here's a step-by-step guide on how to effectively navigate this process:

Data Collection: Begin by collecting a wide range of data related to the local real estate market. Obtain information on recent property sales, listing prices, inventory levels, days on market, and any other relevant metrics.

Utilize Real Estate Databases: Access reputable real estate databases, MLS platforms, and online tools that provide historical and current data about property transactions, price trends, and market activity.

Consult Local Real Estate Agents: Engage with experienced local real estate agents who possess firsthand knowledge of the market. They can provide insights into emerging trends, buyer preferences, and shifts in demand.

Analyze Historical Data: Study historical sales data to identify patterns and cycles in property values. This analysis helps discern seasonal fluctuations, long-term growth trends, and market stability.

Market Segmentation: Divide the market into segments based on property types, neighborhoods, or price ranges. Analyze trends within these segments to understand variations in demand and value.

Inventory Analysis: Assess the current inventory of available properties relative to buyer demand. A low supply of properties often leads to increased competition and upward pressure on prices.

Price Trends: Examine price trends over time to determine whether property values are appreciating, stabilizing, or declining. Look for consistent patterns and anomalies.

Comparative Market Analysis (CMA): Conduct CMAs on a regular basis to gauge how the values of comparable properties have changed over time. Analyze the differences between listing and sale prices.

Local Economic Indicators: Monitor local economic indicators such as job growth, population changes, and development projects. These factors influence housing demand and property values.

Government Policies: Stay informed about zoning changes, building regulations, and any government policies that could impact property development and values.

Media and Reports: Read real estate reports, market analyses, and news articles from reputable sources to gain insights into broader market trends and developments.

Network and Discussions: Engage in conversations with fellow real estate professionals, investors, and industry experts. Participate in local real estate associations or online forums where market trends are discussed.

Attend Real Estate Events: Attend local real estate seminars, workshops, and networking events. These gatherings provide opportunities to learn from experts and gain firsthand insights.

Analytical Tools: Utilize data analysis tools, graphs, and charts to visually represent market trends and patterns. These visuals can aid in identifying shifts and correlations.

Continual Learning: Market trends evolve, so stay updated with ongoing education, training, and industry publications to enhance your understanding of local dynamics.

By following these steps, you can effectively identify and interpret local market trends in residential real estate. This comprehensive approach enables you to make well-informed decisions, adapt to changing market conditions, and navigate the complexities of real estate transactions with confidence.

Impact Of Supply And Demand On Property Values

Supply and demand dynamics exert a significant influence on property values within the real estate market. This fundamental economic relationship plays a pivotal role in shaping how properties are priced and perceived by buyers and sellers.

When demand for properties exceeds the available supply, property values tend to rise. In this scenario, buyers compete for a limited number of properties, driving up prices. This phenomenon is often observed in areas with rapid population growth, strong job markets, and attractive amenities. Elevated demand in such markets can lead to bidding wars, multiple offers, and a sense of urgency among buyers, resulting in upward pressure on property values.

Conversely, when supply outpaces demand, property values may experience a decline. An oversupply of properties can lead to extended days on market, price reductions, and decreased buyer interest. This situation is more likely in areas with excessive construction or economic downturns, where an abundance of available properties can soften demand and prompt sellers to lower prices to attract buyers.

Supply and demand dynamics also influence property types and market segments differently. High demand for certain property types, such as single-family homes or condos, can lead to price appreciation, while oversaturation in other segments, like luxury properties, may exert downward pressure on values.

It's crucial to recognize that supply and demand factors interact with various economic and external influences, shaping the overall market sentiment. Real estate professionals, investors, and consumers closely monitor these dynamics to make informed decisions about buying, selling, and investing in properties. As a result, understanding the delicate balance between supply and demand is essential for comprehending property value fluctuations within the ever-evolving landscape of real estate.

Forecasting Changes That Could Affect ARV

Forecasting changes that could potentially affect the After Repair Value (ARV) in real estate involves considering a range of factors that may influence property values. While the real estate market is inherently dynamic, several key changes can impact ARV projections:

Economic Trends: Shifts in the broader economy, such as fluctuations in interest rates, job growth, inflation, and consumer confidence, can influence buyer demand and purchasing power, consequently affecting ARV.

Market Supply and Demand: Changes in the balance between housing supply and buyer demand can lead to shifts in property values. A shortage of properties can drive up demand and ARV, while an oversupply may exert downward pressure.

Local Development: Infrastructure projects, commercial developments, and neighborhood improvements can enhance an area's desirability and contribute to increased ARV.

Regulatory Changes: Alterations in zoning regulations, building codes, or tax policies can impact property development, demand, and, subsequently, ARV.

Technological Advancements: Technological innovations, such as smart home features and energy-efficient upgrades, can influence property values and ARV by appealing to modern buyer preferences.

Demographic Shifts: Changes in demographics, such as population growth, generational preferences, and household compositions, can drive shifts in demand for certain property types and impact ARV.

Market Sentiment: Changes in consumer sentiment, influenced by factors like media coverage, market speculation, and economic outlook, can affect buyer behavior and ARV.

Environmental Factors: Awareness of climate-related risks, natural disasters, and environmental sustainability can influence property values and shape ARV in vulnerable areas.

Local School Quality: Improvements or declines in local school quality can impact neighborhood desirability, affecting ARV as families seek homes within preferred school districts.

Mortgage Lending Policies: Changes in lending regulations, down payment requirements, and mortgage rates can impact buyer affordability and, consequently, ARV.

Competing Investments: Changes in alternative investment opportunities, such as the stock market or other asset classes, can influence demand for real estate and, in turn, ARV.

Global Events: Global economic events, geopolitical shifts, and health crises (as observed with the COVID-19 pandemic) can have widespread effects on real estate markets and ARV.

Urbanization and Suburbanization: Shifts in population preferences for urban or suburban living can affect property demand and ARV in respective areas.

Interest from Institutional Investors: The influx of institutional investors into certain markets can impact demand, pricing dynamics, and ARV.

Housing Affordability: Changes in income levels, housing affordability, and mortgage accessibility can influence buyer demand and ARV.

Considering these forecasting changes and their potential impacts on ARV empowers real estate professionals, investors, and stakeholders to make informed decisions and adapt strategies within the ever-evolving landscape of real estate valuation.

* * *

CHAPTER 6: CONSIDERING PROPERTY FEATURES AND UPGRADES

How Property Features Affect ARV

Property features play a significant role in influencing the After Repair Value (ARV) of a real estate investment. These features encompass a wide range of physical and aesthetic attributes that contribute to a property's appeal and desirability in the eyes of potential buyers. Here's how property features affect ARV:

Curb Appeal: A well-maintained exterior, landscaping, and curb appeal contribute to a positive first impression, potentially raising the perceived value of the property and its ARV.

Size and Layout: The size and layout of a property, including the number of bedrooms, bathrooms, and overall livable space, directly impact its market value and ARV.

Upgrades and Renovations: Modern and updated features, such as kitchen upgrades, bathroom remodels, energy-efficient appliances, and high-quality finishes, can substantially elevate the ARV by making the property more attractive to buyers.

Amenities: Desirable amenities like swimming pools, outdoor living spaces, decks, and patios can enhance a property's value and justify a higher ARV.

View and Location: Properties with scenic views or prime locations, such as proximity to parks, waterfronts, or vibrant city centers, often command higher ARVs due to their unique appeal.

Energy Efficiency: Energy-efficient features such as solar panels, smart home technology, and efficient HVAC systems can attract environmentally conscious buyers and positively impact ARV.

Storage Space: Ample storage solutions, such as walk-in closets, built-in shelving, and storage rooms, add functionality and contribute to a higher ARV.

Garage and Parking: Availability of covered parking, garages, or dedicated parking spaces can enhance convenience and influence ARV, especially in areas with limited parking options.

Flooring and Finishes: High-quality flooring materials, finishes, and architectural details like crown molding and wainscoting can elevate a property's aesthetics and ARV.

Security and Safety: Features like security systems, gated access, and fire safety measures can instill confidence in buyers and impact ARV positively.

Accessibility: Properties with features catering to accessibility needs, such as ramps, wide doorways, and accessible bathrooms, may appeal to a broader range of buyers and potentially influence ARV.

Historic or Unique Elements: Historic charm, unique architectural elements, or one-of-a-kind design features can create a sense of exclusivity and contribute to a higher perceived value and ARV.

Outdoor Spaces: Attractive outdoor spaces like well-designed gardens, patios, and decks can extend living areas and enhance a property's overall appeal and ARV.

Technology Integration: Integration of smart home technology, including automated lighting, security systems, and entertainment systems, can enhance convenience and impact ARV.

Maintenance and Condition: A property's overall condition and maintenance level significantly influence its perceived value and ARV. Well-maintained properties often command higher prices.

In essence, property features directly influence a property's marketability, buyer appeal, and subsequently, its After Repair Value. Strategic upgrades, renovations, and enhancements to these features can contribute to a higher ARV, making them a crucial consideration for real estate investors, flippers, and homeowners seeking to maximize their returns.

Valuing Renovations And Upgrades Effectively

Effectively valuing renovations and upgrades in residential real estate involves a systematic approach that considers both the costs of improvements and their potential impact on property value. Here's a step-by-step guide to help you navigate this process:

Prioritize Improvements: Begin by identifying and prioritizing the renovations and upgrades that are likely to yield the highest return on investment (ROI). Focus on enhancements that align with market demand and buyer preferences.

Research Costs: Research and estimate the costs associated with each renovation or upgrade. Obtain quotes from contractors, suppliers, and professionals to accurately gauge expenses.

Consult Experts: Seek advice from experienced real estate professionals, appraisers, or contractors who have knowledge of local market trends and can provide insights into which improvements are most impactful.

Comparable Analysis: Conduct a Comparative Market Analysis (CMA) to assess how similar properties with similar improvements have been valued in the market. This can offer insights into potential value appreciation.

Cost-Benefit Analysis: Perform a cost-benefit analysis for each improvement, comparing the estimated cost against the potential increase in property value. Consider both short-term and long-term impacts.

Consider ROI: Prioritize renovations that offer a higher ROI. For example, kitchen and bathroom remodels, curb appeal enhancements, and energy-efficient upgrades often deliver favorable returns.

Market Research: Research the local real estate market to understand buyer preferences and the features that attract higher prices. Tailor your improvements to match market demand.

Assess Market Gap: Identify gaps in the local market where certain features or amenities are lacking. Addressing these gaps through renovations can provide a competitive edge and potentially increase property value.

Appraiser's Perspective: Put yourself in the shoes of an appraiser. Consider how they would assess the value of each improvement based on factors such as quality, functionality, and overall appeal.

Professional Opinions: Consult real estate agents and appraisers to gather their opinions on the potential impact of specific renovations on property value.

Budget and Timeframe: Balance the desired improvements with your budget and timeframe. Some upgrades may require significant investments and time, impacting your overall project goals.

Lifecycle Analysis: Consider the lifecycle of improvements. Evaluate whether certain upgrades, such as a new roof or HVAC system, add long-term value and appeal to potential buyers.

Overimprovement Caution: Be cautious about overimproving beyond the norms of the local market. Renovations that significantly exceed what neighboring properties offer may not yield commensurate returns.

Quality and Workmanship: Focus on quality workmanship and materials. Substandard improvements can have a negative impact on property value and market perception.

Documentation: Keep detailed records of all renovations and upgrades, including receipts, invoices, and before-and-after photos. This documentation can support your claims of value-added improvements.

By diligently following these steps, you can navigate the complex process of valuing renovations and upgrades in residential real estate. This strategic approach ensures that your investment in improvements aligns with market trends, buyer preferences, and the potential to enhance property value.

Calculating ROI On Improvement Projects

Calculating Return on Investment (ROI) for improvement projects in residential real estate requires a systematic approach that considers both the costs of the project and the potential increase in property value. Here's a step-by-step guide to help you accurately assess the ROI of your improvement projects:

Cost Identification: Begin by documenting all costs associated with the improvement project. This includes material expenses, labor costs, permits, design fees, and any other relevant expenses.

Market Research: Research how similar improvement projects have impacted property values in your local real estate market. Look for comparable properties that underwent similar renovations and assess the resulting value increase.

Pre- and Post-Improvement Valuation: Obtain a professional appraisal or work with a real estate agent to determine the current market value of the property before the improvements and an estimated post-improvement value.

Net Gain Calculation: Subtract the total project costs from the projected increase in property value. The result represents the potential net gain from the improvement project.

Calculate ROI: Divide the net gain by the total project costs and multiply by 100 to express the ROI as a percentage.

Holding Period: Consider the expected holding period before selling the property. A shorter holding period may result in a higher annualized ROI.

Resale Costs: Account for transaction costs when selling the property, such as real estate agent commissions, closing costs, and any other fees.

Sensitivity Analysis: Perform sensitivity analysis by testing different scenarios, accounting for potential variations in property value appreciation and project costs.

Opportunity Cost: Assess the opportunity cost of investing in the improvement project compared to alternative investment opportunities.

Risk Assessment: Evaluate potential risks and uncertainties, such as unexpected expenses or changes in market conditions, and factor these into your ROI calculation.

Financing Considerations: If you're financing the project, incorporate interest costs and loan terms into your ROI analysis.

Long-Term Impact: Consider the long-term impact of improvements on property maintenance, future resale value, and potential rental income if applicable.

Professional Input: Consult with experienced real estate professionals, appraisers, or financial advisors to validate your calculations and gain insights into market trends.

Regular Review: Continuously monitor the progress of the project and track changes in property value over time. Update your ROI calculations periodically to ensure accuracy.

Realistic Expectations: Maintain realistic expectations for your improvement project's impact on property value. Not all renovations yield equal returns, so prioritize projects that align with market demand and buyer preferences.

By following these steps, you can effectively calculate the Return on Investment for improvement projects in residential real estate. This analytical approach empowers you to make informed decisions, prioritize projects with favorable ROI prospects, and maximize the financial benefits of your real estate endeavors.

* * *

CHAPTER 7: HANDLING SPECIAL CASES AND CHALLENGES

Dealing With Unique Property Types

Dealing with unique property types in real estate requires a strategic and adaptable approach to effectively navigate the distinct challenges and opportunities they present. Here's a step-by-step guide to help you handle unique property types:

Thorough Research: Begin by conducting comprehensive research to understand the specific characteristics and nuances of the unique property type. Gather information about its history, architectural features, market demand, and any legal or zoning considerations.

Expert Consultation: Seek advice from real estate professionals, appraisers, and experts who specialize in the particular property type. Their insights can provide valuable guidance on pricing, marketing, and potential challenges.

Market Analysis: Analyze the local real estate market to assess the demand for similar unique properties. Determine whether there is a niche market or specific buyer segment that would be interested in the property.

Comparable Properties: Identify comparable properties, even if they are rare, that share similar unique characteristics. Look for recent sales or listings to gauge how these properties are valued in the market.

Customized Marketing: Develop a targeted marketing strategy that highlights the distinctive features and benefits of the property. Emphasize what sets it apart and appeals to potential buyers seeking a unique living experience.

Educate Buyers: Be prepared to educate potential buyers about the property's unique attributes, potential uses, and any considerations they should be aware of. Provide clear and transparent information to address any questions or concerns.

Appropriate Pricing: Price the property based on a combination of market data, comparable properties, and the perceived value of its uniqueness. Consider consulting with an appraiser to ensure accurate pricing.

Legal and Zoning Compliance: Ensure that the property complies with all local zoning regulations and legal requirements. Address any potential issues upfront to avoid complications during the transaction process.

Highlight Potential: Showcase the potential of the unique property. If it requires renovations or updates, present design concepts or renovation ideas that can help buyers envision its transformation.

Network within Niche: Connect with individuals or organizations that have an interest in or connection to the unique property type. Attend relevant events, join online forums, and engage with niche communities to expand your reach.

Patience and Flexibility: Understand that selling or valuing a unique property may take longer than traditional properties. Be patient and flexible in your approach, and be prepared to adapt your strategy as needed.

Appreciate Uniqueness: Embrace the uniqueness of the property and leverage it as a selling point. Highlight how it offers a one-of-a-kind living experience that can't be easily replicated.

Professional Marketing Materials: Invest in high-quality marketing materials, including professional photos, videos, and descriptions that effectively convey the property's unique features and charm.

Negotiation Skills: Be prepared for negotiations, as buyers may have specific requests or concerns related to the unique aspects of the property. Skilled negotiation can help bridge any gaps.

Stay Informed: Continuously stay informed about market trends, buyer preferences, and any changes that may impact the demand for unique property types. Stay adaptable and open to adjusting your approach accordingly.

By following these steps, you can navigate the complexities of dealing with unique property types in real estate, capitalize on their distinct appeal, and effectively connect with the right buyers who appreciate their individuality.

Estimating ARV For Distressed Properties

Estimating the After Repair Value (ARV) for distressed properties requires a careful and methodical approach due to the unique challenges and considerations involved. Here's a step-by-step guide to help you effectively estimate ARV for distressed properties:

Property Inspection: Begin by conducting a thorough inspection of the distressed property. Identify the extent of repairs needed, structural issues, and any safety concerns. Take detailed notes and photographs to assess the overall condition.

Comparable Analysis: Research recent sales of comparable properties in the same neighborhood or vicinity. Look for distressed properties that have been renovated and sold to determine their post-repair values.

Adjustments: Analyze the differences between the distressed property and the comparable renovated properties. Make adjustments for factors such as square footage, number of bedrooms and bathrooms, lot size, and overall condition.

Renovation Costs: Estimate the costs of necessary repairs and renovations. Obtain quotes from contractors or use reliable cost estimation tools to calculate expenses for bringing the property to marketable condition.

Potential ARV: Add the estimated renovation costs to the adjusted value of the distressed property. This provides a preliminary estimate of the potential ARV after repairs are completed.

Market Trends: Consider current market trends and conditions. Evaluate whether there is demand for renovated distressed properties in the area and how they have been performing in terms of sale prices.

Investor's Margin: Account for your desired profit margin or return on investment. Ensure that the estimated ARV leaves room for profit after factoring in all costs and potential contingencies.

Consult Professionals: Seek advice from experienced real estate agents, appraisers, or investors who have expertise in distressed properties. Their insights can provide a more accurate perspective on estimating ARV.

Local Regulations: Be aware of local regulations, zoning requirements, and permit processes that may impact the timeline and cost of renovations.

Risk Assessment: Evaluate potential risks and challenges associated with renovating distressed properties, such as unforeseen repairs, delays, or changes in market conditions.

Multiple Scenarios: Consider different scenarios based on varying levels of renovation. Estimate ARV for both minimal repairs and a more extensive renovation to understand the potential range of outcomes.

Professional Appraisal: If feasible, consider obtaining a professional appraisal that takes into account the property's current distressed condition and estimates its value after repairs.

Financial Analysis: Perform a financial analysis that includes a detailed breakdown of all costs, potential revenues, and projected profits. This analysis provides a comprehensive view of the investment's viability.

Due Diligence: Engage in thorough due diligence to uncover any hidden issues or challenges that could impact the renovation process and final ARV.

Contingency Plan: Have a contingency plan in place for unexpected expenses or challenges that may arise during the renovation process. Building in a safety net can help protect your investment.

By following these steps, you can navigate the intricacies of estimating ARV for distressed properties and make informed decisions that optimize your investment potential.

Addressing Complex Scenarios And Limitations

Addressing complex scenarios and limitations when evaluating property in After Repair Value (ARV) requires a comprehensive and adaptive approach. Here's a step-by-step guide to help you effectively navigate these challenges:

Thorough Research: Begin by conducting thorough research on the property and its unique complexities. Understand any historical or structural factors that could impact its value.

Consult Experts: Seek guidance from experienced real estate professionals, appraisers, contractors, or engineers who can provide insights into addressing complex scenarios and limitations.

Comparable Analysis: Conduct a detailed comparative analysis of similar properties that have undergone similar renovations or have faced comparable limitations. Analyze how these properties were valued post-repairs.

Scenario Analysis: Consider multiple scenarios based on different levels of repairs, renovations, or limitations. Estimate ARV for each scenario to understand the potential range of outcomes.

Creative Solutions: Explore creative solutions to address limitations. For example, if there are zoning restrictions, consider alternative use options or adaptive reuse that could enhance the property's value.

Value-Added Features: Identify value-added features that could help offset limitations. Highlight unique selling points that could attract buyers despite the property's challenges.

Renovation Strategies: Develop renovation strategies that focus on addressing the property's limitations while maximizing its potential. Prioritize improvements that have the most impact.

Local Market Trends: Analyze current market trends and buyer preferences in the local area. Understand how buyers perceive and value properties with similar limitations.

Customized Marketing: Craft a tailored marketing strategy that highlights the property's potential and emphasizes its strengths. Showcase how the limitations can be overcome or turned into advantages.

Financial Analysis: Perform a detailed financial analysis that includes all costs, potential revenues, and projected profits for each scenario. Evaluate whether the investment is financially viable considering the limitations.

Expert Appraisal: Consider obtaining a professional appraisal that takes into account the property's complexities and limitations. An expert appraiser can provide an objective assessment of its value.

Legal Considerations: Ensure compliance with all legal and regulatory requirements related to the property's limitations. Address any necessary permits or approvals.

Contingency Planning: Develop a robust contingency plan to manage unexpected challenges that may arise during renovations. Having a plan in place helps mitigate risks.

Flexibility: Remain flexible and open to adapting your strategy as new information emerges. Adjust your approach based on market feedback, expert advice, and changing conditions.

Transparency: Be transparent with potential buyers about the property's limitations and the steps taken to address them. Providing clear information builds trust and credibility.

By following these steps, you can effectively address complex scenarios and limitations when evaluating property in ARV. This approach empowers you to make informed decisions, find innovative solutions, and optimize the property's value despite its challenges.

* * *

CHAPTER 8: THE ROLE OF APPRAISALS

Understanding The Appraisal Process And Its Connection To ARV

Understanding the appraisal process and its connection to After Repair Value (ARV) is crucial for accurately assessing a property's value, especially in the context of real estate investment and renovation. Here's a step-by-step guide to help you grasp the appraisal process and its relationship to ARV:

Appraisal Basics: Begin by familiarizing yourself with the fundamentals of property appraisal. An appraisal is a professional assessment of a property's value conducted by a certified appraiser. It involves evaluating various factors that influence value, including location, condition, size, features, and recent comparable sales.

Appraiser's Role: Gain insights into the role of an appraiser. Appraisers are trained professionals who provide an unbiased and objective estimate of a property's value based on thorough analysis and industry standards.

Appraisal Methods: Explore the primary appraisal methods used by appraisers: the Sales Comparison Approach, Income Approach, and Cost Approach. Understand how these methods are applied to determine a property's value.

Comparable Sales: Recognize the importance of comparable sales (comps) in both the appraisal process and ARV calculation. Appraisers use recently sold properties with similar characteristics to the subject property to establish its value.

Property Inspection: Learn about the property inspection phase of the appraisal process. Appraisers physically inspect the property to assess its condition, layout, features, and any improvements or repairs needed.

Market Analysis: Understand how appraisers analyze market trends, supply and demand, and local economic factors to contextualize a property's value within the current real estate market.

Connection to ARV: Recognize the connection between the appraisal process and ARV. ARV represents the estimated value of a property after renovations, and it is often influenced by comparable sales and the analysis conducted by appraisers.

Renovation Consideration: Appreciate how appraisers factor in the value of renovations when assessing ARV. Appraisers consider the impact of improvements on a property's value, helping investors understand the potential return on their renovation investment.

Data Utilization: Gain insights into the data sources and tools appraisers use to gather information about the subject property, comparable sales, and market trends. These sources contribute to informed valuation decisions.

Appraisal Report: Understand the components of an appraisal report, including the property's description, comparable sales analysis, valuation methods used, and the final estimated value.

Investor Insights: Recognize that understanding the appraisal process enhances an investor's ability to interpret and leverage appraisals when evaluating ARV for investment properties.

Collaboration with Appraisers: Consider building relationships with appraisers who specialize in your target market. Their expertise and insights can provide valuable guidance when estimating ARV.

Documentation: Appreciate the importance of maintaining detailed documentation of property improvements, renovations, and any unique features that could impact ARV. This information can support appraisal accuracy.

Market Fluctuations: Acknowledge that market conditions can impact both appraised values and ARV. Understanding market dynamics helps investors anticipate potential fluctuations in property values.

Continuous Learning: Stay informed about changes in appraisal regulations, industry standards, and market trends. Ongoing education ensures your understanding of the appraisal process remains current and relevant.

By following these steps, you can develop a comprehensive understanding of the appraisal process and its integral connection to estimating ARV. This knowledge empowers you to make informed investment decisions and navigate the complexities of real estate valuation more effectively.

Leveraging Appraisals For Accurate ARV Estimation

Leveraging appraisals for accurate After Repair Value (ARV) estimation involves a strategic approach that capitalizes on the insights provided by professional appraisers to enhance your property valuation. Here's a step-by-step guide to effectively utilize appraisals for precise ARV estimation:

Select Qualified Appraisers: Choose certified and experienced appraisers who are familiar with the local real estate market and have expertise in assessing properties similar to the one you're evaluating. Their knowledge is instrumental in generating reliable ARV estimates.

Provide Comprehensive Information: Furnish appraisers with comprehensive details about the property and your renovation plans.

Highlight any upgrades, improvements, or unique features that can impact the property's value.

Discuss ARV Objective: Clearly communicate your intention to estimate the property's ARV for investment purposes. This helps the appraiser tailor their analysis to align with your specific goals.

Appraisal Report Analysis: Carefully review the appraisal report once it's completed. Pay close attention to the appraiser's assessment of the property's condition, features, and any improvements considered in the valuation process.

Comparable Sales Selection: Examine the comparable sales (comps) used by the appraiser in the report. Compare these comps with your own research to ensure they accurately reflect the post-repair condition and improvements.

Adjustment Evaluation: Assess any adjustments made by the appraiser to account for differences between the subject property and the comps. Scrutinize these adjustments to validate their accuracy and relevance to your ARV estimation.

Engage in Dialogue: Initiate a constructive dialogue with the appraiser if you have questions or concerns about their methodology, comparable selection, or adjustments. A collaborative approach can lead to a more accurate ARV assessment.

Incorporate Renovation Costs: Factor in your estimated renovation costs and improvements to the appraiser's assessment. Discuss how these upgrades contribute to the property's post-repair value.

Seek Professional Insights: Consult real estate professionals or investors who specialize in the local market. Their input can provide a broader perspective on how appraisals align with ARV estimates.

Market Trends Interpretation: Analyze the appraiser's interpretation of current market trends and conditions. Understand how these trends influence the property's value and potential ARV.

Legal and Regulatory Compliance: Ensure the appraisal report adheres to all legal and regulatory requirements. A compliant report enhances its credibility and relevance to your ARV estimation.

Future Valuation Factors: Discuss with the appraiser any factors that could influence the property's value in the future, such as planned developments, infrastructure projects, or changing neighborhood dynamics.

Long-Term Investment Strategy: Align your ARV estimation with your long-term investment strategy. Consider the potential appreciation and market performance over time when incorporating the appraiser's insights.

Document Improvements: Maintain detailed documentation of all improvements and renovations made to the property. This documentation can support the accuracy of your ARV estimation and future appraisals.

Continuous Learning: Stay informed about evolving appraisal methodologies, market trends, and best practices. Ongoing education enhances your ability to effectively leverage appraisals for precise ARV estimation.

By following these steps, you can harness the expertise of appraisers to refine your ARV estimation process. This collaborative and analytical approach empowers you to make well-informed investment decisions and maximize the accuracy of your property valuation assessments.

Collaborating With Appraisers Effectively

Collaborating effectively with real estate appraisers requires clear communication, mutual respect, and a shared understanding of the property's value. Here's a step-by-step guide to establish a productive collaboration with real estate appraisers:

Choose Qualified Appraisers: Select experienced and certified appraisers who specialize in the property type and market you're dealing with. Their expertise enhances the accuracy of the valuation process.

Set Clear Objectives: Define your objectives and expectations for the appraisal. Clearly communicate your purpose, whether it's estimating ARV for investment, refinancing, or other purposes.

Provide Comprehensive Information: Furnish appraisers with detailed information about the property, including its features, condition, recent improvements, and renovation plans. The more they know, the more accurate their assessment will be.

Engage Early: Involve appraisers early in the process, even before renovations begin. Their insights can guide your renovation decisions and potential impact on property value.

Open Dialogue: Initiate a dialogue with the appraiser to discuss your investment strategy, goals, and renovation plans. Share your insights and listen to their professional opinions.

Access to Property: Facilitate appraiser access to the property for inspections and assessments. Provide any relevant documentation or permits they may need.

Share Comparable Research: Offer your own research on comparable properties and recent sales, demonstrating your understanding of the local market. Discuss how these comparables align with your ARV estimation.

Review Appraisal Process: Seek to understand the appraiser's methodology, selection of comparable properties, and adjustments made. Ask questions to clarify any aspects of the process you're unsure about.

Highlight Improvements: Emphasize the specific improvements and renovations you've made to the property. Explain how these enhancements contribute to its post-repair value.

Respect Professional Judgment: Respect the appraiser's professional judgment and independence. While you can share insights, remember that they must maintain objectivity in their assessment.

Discuss Limitations: Openly discuss any limitations or challenges associated with the property. Addressing these issues upfront allows the appraiser to consider them in their valuation.

Collaborate on Adjustments: Collaborate with the appraiser on adjustments for differences between the subject property and comparables. Share your perspective on the significance of these adjustments.

Attend Appraisal Inspection: Whenever possible, attend the property inspection with the appraiser. This allows you to provide context, answer questions, and showcase improvements.

Feedback and Clarification: Review the appraisal report thoroughly. If you have feedback or need clarification, communicate your concerns in a respectful and constructive manner.

Long-Term Relationship: Cultivate a long-term relationship with appraisers who understand your investment approach. A consistent collaboration can lead to more accurate valuations over time.

By following these steps, you can establish a positive and collaborative working relationship with real estate appraisers. Effective collaboration enhances the accuracy of your property valuations, ensures alignment with your investment goals, and contributes to informed decision-making.

* * *

CHAPTER 9: FINE-TUNING YOUR ARV ESTIMATION SKILLS

Continuous Learning And Staying Updated On Market Trends

Continuous learning and staying updated on real estate market trends are essential practices for success in the real estate industry. Here's why they are important:

Market Dynamics: Real estate markets are dynamic and can experience fluctuations due to economic, social, and regulatory changes. Staying informed about market trends helps you anticipate shifts and make timely decisions.

Informed Decision-Making: Up-to-date knowledge enables you to make informed investment, pricing, and strategy decisions. You can adapt your approach based on current market conditions to maximize returns.

Risk Mitigation: Being aware of market trends helps you identify and mitigate potential risks. Understanding factors that influence supply, demand, and property values allows you to assess risks more accurately.

Identifying Opportunities: Market trends reveal emerging opportunities, such as up-and-coming neighborhoods, property types in demand, or new investment strategies. Staying updated helps you capitalize on these trends.

Competitive Edge: In a competitive market, staying ahead of trends gives you a competitive edge. You can position yourself as an expert who offers valuable insights to clients, partners, and stakeholders.

Networking: Being knowledgeable about market trends enhances your ability to connect with other industry professionals. Engaging in meaningful discussions about current trends fosters valuable relationships.

Adaptability: Continuous learning allows you to adapt to changing market dynamics. You can refine your strategies, adjust your investment focus, and align with shifting buyer preferences.

ARV Accuracy: Accurate ARV estimation relies on understanding market trends. This knowledge helps you make precise assessments and improves the success of your investment ventures.

Long-Term Planning: Staying updated helps you develop effective long-term plans. You can anticipate the direction of the market and plan investments that align with future trends.

Client Trust: Clients and partners trust professionals who demonstrate a strong grasp of market trends. Your ability to provide accurate insights enhances your credibility and builds trust.

Regulatory Changes: Real estate is subject to regulatory changes and policies that impact property values and transactions. Staying informed helps you navigate legal complexities and compliance requirements.

Optimized Strategy: With knowledge of current trends, you can optimize your investment and sales strategies to align with what buyers are seeking in the market.

Financial Management: Staying updated allows you to make sound financial decisions, allocate resources effectively, and manage cash flow based on anticipated market conditions.

Maximize Returns: By understanding market trends, you can time your investments for optimal returns. This knowledge helps you buy, renovate, and sell properties when market conditions are favorable.

Industry Credibility: Continuous learning demonstrates your commitment to professional growth and positions you as a respected authority in the real estate field.

In summary, continuous learning and staying updated on real estate market trends are crucial for making informed decisions, minimizing risks, identifying opportunities, and achieving success in the ever-evolving real estate landscape.

Refining Your Estimation Techniques Over Time

Refining your After Repair Value (ARV) estimation techniques over time involves a combination of learning, practice, feedback, and adaptation. Here's a step-by-step guide to help you enhance your ARV estimation skills:

Continuous Learning: Stay updated on real estate market trends, property valuation methodologies, and local market dynamics. Attend seminars, workshops, online courses, and read industry publications to expand your knowledge.

Analyze Past Deals: Review your past investment deals and compare your initial ARV estimates with the actual sale prices. Analyze the discrepancies to identify patterns, areas for improvement, and potential factors that influenced the outcomes.

Gather Feedback: Seek feedback from experienced real estate professionals, appraisers, mentors, or colleagues. Their insights can provide valuable perspectives on your estimation techniques and help you identify blind spots.

Refine Comparable Analysis: Sharpen your skills in selecting and analyzing comparable properties. Develop a systematic approach to identifying comps, making adjustments, and assessing their relevance to the subject property.

Renovation Impact: Deepen your understanding of how specific renovations and improvements impact property value. Study case studies, consult experts, and analyze before-and-after scenarios to enhance your assessment.

Use Data Analytics: Leverage real estate data platforms and tools to access comprehensive market data, sales histories, and property trends. Data-driven analysis can provide more accurate insights into ARV estimation.

Scenario Analysis: Practice estimating ARV for different renovation scenarios. This exercise helps you evaluate the potential impact of various improvements on property value and hones your estimation skills.

Comparative Market Analysis (CMA): Develop expertise in conducting thorough CMAs to identify trends, pricing patterns, and buyer preferences in your local market. This informs your ARV estimation strategy.

Software and Tools: Explore ARV calculation software or spreadsheets that streamline the process and help you make adjustments more effectively.

Incorporate Feedback: Apply feedback received from real estate professionals, appraisers, and colleagues to fine-tune your estimation techniques.

Collaborate with Appraisers: Collaborate with appraisers on projects whenever possible. Learn from their methodology, ask questions, and gain insights into their approach to property valuation.

Market Research: Invest time in thorough market research to understand how economic, demographic, and neighborhood factors influence property values. This knowledge enhances the accuracy of your ARV estimates.

Networking: Engage with other real estate investors, attend industry events, and participate in forums to share experiences, learn from peers, and gain insights into effective ARV estimation strategies.

Track Record: Keep a record of your ARV estimates and the subsequent sale prices of properties. Analyzing this historical data can reveal trends and areas where adjustments are needed.

Adapt and Evolve: As market conditions change and your experience grows, be open to adapting your estimation techniques. Stay flexible and willing to adjust your approach based on new information and insights.

By consistently applying these strategies and dedicating time to refining your ARV estimation techniques, you'll develop a stronger ability to accurately assess property values, make informed investment decisions, and achieve greater success in real estate.

Avoiding Common Pitfalls And Mistakes

Avoiding common pitfalls and mistakes in estimating After Repair Value (ARV) is crucial for making accurate investment decisions. Here's a step-by-step guide to help you steer clear of pitfalls and enhance your ARV estimation process:

Thorough Property Inspection: Conduct a comprehensive property inspection to identify any hidden issues, structural problems, or major repairs needed. Underestimating necessary repairs can lead to inaccurate ARV estimates.

Selecting Inaccurate Comps: Choose comparable properties (comps) that closely match the subject property in terms of location, size, condition, and features. Using irrelevant or outdated comps can lead to skewed estimations.

Neglecting Renovation Costs: Accurately assess the costs of renovations and improvements needed to bring the property to marketable condition. Underestimating renovation expenses can result in an inflated ARV estimate.

Overestimating Value-Adding Features: Be realistic about the impact of value-added features and renovations on the property's ARV. Not all improvements yield a proportional increase in value.

Market Trends Ignorance: Stay informed about current market trends, buyer preferences, and neighborhood dynamics. Ignoring market trends can lead to inaccurate ARV estimations that don't align with demand.

Ignoring Zoning and Regulations: Be aware of local zoning restrictions, building codes, and regulations that could affect the property's value. Failing to consider these factors can lead to inaccurate ARV estimates.

Rushing the Estimation Process: Take your time to gather accurate data, analyze comps, and assess renovation costs. Rushing through the estimation process can result in errors and oversights.

Lack of Professional Advice: Consult experienced real estate professionals, appraisers, or mentors to validate your ARV estimations. Their expertise can help you avoid common pitfalls.

Emotional Bias: Avoid letting personal preferences or emotions influence your ARV estimation. Base your assessment on objective data and market analysis.

Exaggerating Property Improvements: Be transparent about the scope and quality of renovations. Exaggerating improvements can lead to unrealistic ARV estimations.

Neglecting Local Market Variations: Consider variations in property values within different neighborhoods or micro-markets. Ignoring localized trends can lead to inaccurate estimations.

Overlooking External Factors: Evaluate external factors such as economic conditions, interest rates, and job growth that impact property demand and value. Neglecting these factors can lead to flawed estimations.

Lack of Data Validation: Verify the accuracy of data sources, including property records, recent sales data, and renovation costs. Relying on outdated or incorrect information can lead to errors.

Overconfidence: Avoid overestimating your ability to accurately predict market trends and property values. Be open to seeking input and refining your estimation techniques.

Not Adjusting for Differences: Ensure that adjustments for differences between comps and the subject property are accurate and supported by market evidence. Incorrect adjustments can distort the ARV estimate.

By being diligent, thorough, and mindful of potential pitfalls, you can enhance the accuracy of your ARV estimations, make informed investment decisions, and navigate the real estate market more successfully.

* * *

CHAPTER 10: APPLYING ARV IN REAL ESTATE VENTURES

Integrating ARV Estimation Into Investment Decisions

Integrating After Repair Value (ARV) estimation into your investment decisions is a critical step to ensure informed and profitable real estate ventures. Here's a comprehensive guide on how to effectively incorporate ARV estimation into your investment process:

Initial Property Assessment: Begin by conducting a thorough assessment of the property's current condition, features, and potential for improvements. Identify the scope of renovations needed to enhance its value.

Gather Data: Collect data on comparable properties (comps) that have recently sold in the same neighborhood or vicinity. Focus on properties that are similar in size, condition, and features to the subject property.

Renovation Costs: Estimate the costs of necessary renovations and improvements. This includes repairs, upgrades, and any value-added features that can enhance the property's appeal to potential buyers.

Calculate ARV: Combine the adjusted value of the subject property based on comps with the estimated renovation costs. This provides an initial ARV estimate that reflects the property's potential post-repair value.

Market Analysis: Analyze current market trends, buyer preferences, and demand in the local area. Consider factors such as supply and demand, neighborhood desirability, and economic conditions that could impact the property's future value.

Investment Goals: Align your ARV estimation with your investment goals. Determine your desired profit margin and return on investment (ROI) to ensure the project meets your financial objectives.

Risk Assessment: Evaluate potential risks and challenges associated with the investment. Consider factors such as market volatility, potential delays in renovations, and unforeseen costs.

Multiple Scenarios: Explore different renovation scenarios and their potential impact on ARV. Calculate ARV estimates for varying levels of improvements to assess the range of potential outcomes.

Financial Analysis: Perform a comprehensive financial analysis that includes all costs (acquisition, renovations, holding, selling), potential revenues, and projected profits. Evaluate whether the investment aligns with your financial strategy.

Exit Strategy: Determine your exit strategy, whether it's selling the property after renovations, renting it out, or using it for other purposes. Your ARV estimation should support your chosen exit strategy.

Contingency Planning: Develop contingency plans for unexpected challenges that may arise during the renovation process. Build a safety net into your financial analysis to account for potential setbacks.

Expert Consultation: Seek advice from experienced real estate professionals, appraisers, contractors, or mentors. Their insights can provide valuable guidance and help you refine your ARV estimation.

Due Diligence: Conduct thorough due diligence to verify property details, data accuracy, and market information. Ensure that your ARV estimation is based on reliable and up-to-date information.

Document Improvements: Keep detailed records of all improvements and renovations made to the property. Documenting these changes supports the accuracy of your ARV estimation and future appraisals.

Regular Review: Continuously review and update your ARV estimates as market conditions change, renovations progress, and additional information becomes available.

By following these steps, you can seamlessly integrate ARV estimation into your investment decisions, make well-informed choices, and maximize the potential for successful and profitable real estate investments.

Negotiation Strategies Based On ARV Insights

Utilizing negotiation strategies based on After Repair Value (ARV) insights can help you achieve favorable outcomes in real estate transactions. Here are some effective negotiation strategies that leverage ARV insights:

Knowledge-Based Approach: Use your ARV estimation as a foundation for informed negotiations. Present data-backed insights about the property's potential post-repair value to support your negotiation position.

Anchor High: Begin negotiations by anchoring the discussion around the property's ARV. Emphasize the value that your improvements and renovations will bring, setting a higher starting point for price negotiations.

Value-Add Proposition: Highlight the specific improvements and enhancements you plan to make to the property. Convey how these upgrades will contribute to a higher ARV and justify your proposed price.

Comparison with Comps: Compare your ARV estimation with recent sales of comparable properties in the area. Show how your offer aligns with market trends and supports your negotiation position.

Seller's Perspective: Understand the seller's motivations and concerns. If your ARV estimation demonstrates a higher value than the seller's asking price, use this insight to negotiate a more favorable deal.

Win-Win Approach: Position your negotiation as a win-win scenario. Explain how your ARV insights benefit both parties by helping the seller achieve a higher sale price and you realizing a profitable investment.

Renovation Costs: Present your estimated renovation costs and explain how these expenses are factored into your offer. Demonstrating transparency can build trust and support your negotiation position.

Contingencies: Use ARV insights to justify any contingencies you include in the offer, such as inspections, repairs, or obtaining specific permits. Explain how these contingencies align with the property's potential value.

Future Value: Discuss the potential appreciation and market performance of the property based on your ARV estimation. Highlight the long-term value you foresee, which can strengthen your negotiation position.

Offer Flexibility: Structure your offer with flexibility that considers the property's ARV potential. For example, offer a higher purchase price contingent on achieving the projected post-repair value.

Competitive Advantage: If there are competing offers, leverage your ARV insights to showcase the value you bring as an investor who understands the property's potential and can close the deal efficiently.

Escalation Clause: Consider using an escalation clause that automatically increases your offer if another buyer makes a higher bid. Your ARV insights can provide a solid basis for setting the escalation terms.

Time-Sensitive Offers: Emphasize the time-sensitive nature of your offer, especially if your ARV estimation demonstrates a substantial increase in value after renovations. This urgency can prompt the seller to negotiate more favorably.

Build Rapport: Develop a positive rapport with the seller by sharing your ARV insights in a respectful and collaborative manner. Establishing a connection can enhance the negotiation process.

Walk-Away Point: Determine your walk-away point based on your ARV estimation and financial goals. If negotiations don't align with your investment strategy, be prepared to walk away and explore other opportunities.

By integrating these negotiation strategies based on ARV insights, you can enhance your negotiation skills, build stronger arguments, and increase the likelihood of achieving favorable terms in real estate transactions.

CONCLUSION

In conclusion, mastering the art of estimating After Repair Value (ARV) is a transformative skill that sets seasoned real estate professionals apart. Throughout this book, we've embarked on a comprehensive journey through the intricacies of ARV estimation, exploring a spectrum of techniques, methodologies, and strategies used by industry experts.

Armed with a deep understanding of property valuation, the critical role of market analysis, and the impact of renovations, you now possess a toolbox of insights to confidently navigate the dynamic landscape of real estate investments. By leveraging ARV like the pros, you've gained the power to make informed decisions, seize opportunities, and optimize returns on your ventures.

Our exploration has illuminated the significance of accurate comparables selection, the delicate art of adjustments, and the judicious incorporation of market trends. Through case studies, anecdotes, and practical exercises, you've internalized the principles that underpin successful ARV estimation, and you're poised to apply this knowledge with finesse.

Remember that while the journey of mastering ARV estimation is enriching, it is also a continuous endeavor. The real estate landscape evolves, market dynamics shift, and new investment strategies emerge. As you embark on your own professional journey, embrace the ethos of lifelong learning, staying attuned to the pulse of local markets, and refining your ARV estimation techniques.

Armed with the tools, insights, and wisdom shared in these pages, you're equipped to confidently estimate ARV like the pros. Whether you're a seasoned investor looking to fine-tune your strategies or a newcomer seeking to navigate the real estate realm with finesse, the knowledge you've acquired here is your compass on the path to successful property valuation.

As you embark on your future investment endeavors, may your ARV estimations be accurate, your ventures prosperous, and your impact on the real estate world enduring. Here's to a future of shrewd estimations, wise investments, and a journey marked by prosperity and success.

And as an added bonux, scan the QR code below and get a lifetime 10% coupon for t-shirt purchase. Simply apply the code BOOK at checkout.